Calamy Celebrated

The 350th Anniversary of the birth of Dr Edmund Calamy (1671–1732)

The Champion of Nonconformity

A faithful servant of Jesus Christ in depressing times, this forgotten hero inspires hope in our dark days.

BY ALAN C. CLIFFORD

H&E
Publishing

Andrew Fuller
CENTER *for* BAPTIST STUDIES
at THE SOUTHERN BAPTIST THEOLOGICAL SEMINARY

Calamy Celebrated: The Champion of Nonconformity
© 2021 Alan C. Clifford

Published by: H&E Publishing, Peterborough, Ontario / The Andrew Fuller
Center for Baptist Studies, Louisville, Kentucky

www.hesedandemet.com
www.andrewfullercenter.org

Design and layout: Quinta Press (quintapress.com)

Paperback ISBN: 978-1-77484-022-1

E-book ISBN: 978-1-77484-025-2

First edition, 2021

Commendation

This very welcome account of Edmund Calamy has Alan Clifford's characteristic clarity and forcefulness—that is, commitment—coupled with, again characteristically, an unrivalled familiarity with the primary sources. Its summary of the context and course of Calamy's life draws out clearly his character and significance, and accords this unduly neglected figure his true place and standing in the history of dissent. The rehabilitation of Calamy's *Divine Mercy Exalted* is especially persuasive. And all this is done with a liveliness and wit too rare in scholarly writing.

Neil Keeble
Emeritus Professor of English Studies, University of Stirling

DEDICATION

On the centenary of his birth, I dedicate this publication to the memory my doctoral tutor, the Revd Dr R. Tudur Jones (1921–98), formerly Principal of Coleg Bala-Bangor, and Honorary Professor in the School of Theology and Religious Studies, the University College of North Wales, Bangor, Gwynedd, North Wales. He kindly endorsed the theological analysis and conclusions of my doctoral thesis, conclusions which inform the perspective of the following work. The thesis was eventually published by Oxford University Press in 1990,[1] a copy being presented to 'Dr Tudur' in appreciation of his guidance and help. In the Preface, I wrote:

Believing that I had the best tutor available in 'Dr Tudur' (as his students affectionately address him), I will always be grateful to him for his knowledge, wisdom, and kindness. He was always just and generous in assessing my work. Since I was in pastoral charge of a Norfolk village church—I was a part-time, external student—Dr Tudur's prompt and encouraging postal responses to my efforts were all the more important.

In his letter of thanks of 9 April 1991 (which remains a precious document in my possession), he wrote:

Dear Alan: it was most kind of you to present me with a copy of your book. It is an impressive and attractive volume. I shall treasure it, not only for its admirable contents, but as a reminder of the pleasure I had supervising your research. I sincerely hope that it sells well, as it deserves to do.

But above all, I am deeply moved by your gracious references to me in your "Preface". I hardly deserve what you say. Many, many thanks.

I trust that the family flourishes and that you feel your ministry is being blessed.

With cordial Christian greetings,

Yours appreciatively,

Tudur.

---

1   Alan C. Clifford, *Atonement and Justification: English Evangelical Theology 1640–1790—An Evaluation* (Clarendon Press, Oxford, 1990).

Es. E. Calamy.

INTRODUCTION

Apart from modest attention from nonconformist scholars (Dr Tudur Jones being an exception),[2] Dr Calamy is a largely unsung hero of a depressing period in English church history. While he never had the impact of his hero Richard Baxter (and how many could claim that until George Whitefield appeared in 1735?), Calamy shared most of Baxter's convictions, a good deal of his piety and an equally-strong pastoral and evangelistic commitment. In addition, besides documenting the sacrifice of the ejected ministers of 1662, he perhaps more than any other preacher and theologian transmitted Baxter's wonderful legacy to the eighteenth century and beyond. At a time when frequently-persecuted Protestant Dissent struggled to justify its existence within late Stuart and early Hanoverian society, Dr David Wykes points out that Calamy emerged as the 'Champion of Nonconformity'.[3] His own fascinating autobiography illuminates the period in which he lived. For these reasons, we do well to explore the life and labours of Dr Edmund Calamy.

CALAMY'S LAND

The England of Calamy's day was fast becoming a political, social, moral and religious wilderness. Reaction to Puritan morality could be witnessed in every realm of life. Popular with the intellectuals was Deism, a system of thought which rejected both the supernatural and a supernatural, personal God. The Deists replaced the study of revealed theology by the study of natural theology, arguing that all that needed to be known about God could be derived from a scientific study of the created order. The Deists were not atheists in the strict sense; they believed in a God who was the 'first cause' of the universe, but they rejected the personal God of the Bible. The Deists viewed God like a watchmaker who, having made and wound up the watch, leaves it to run down without any further involvement on His part. Deism stood for the authority of reason at the expense of revelation, and its

---

2   See R. Tudur Jones, *Congregationalism in England* (London: Independent Press, 1962), 84, 134–5, 138, 169, 183.

3   David. L. Wykes, 'Calamy, Edmund (1671–1732)', *Oxford Dictionary of National Biography* (Oxford University Press, 2004).

advocates preached morality rather than religion. Calamy himself lamented, 'Are not too many among us so weary of revelation, as to be willing to return back to natural religion, or Deism?'[4]

Reactions to the new liberalism, incongruously styled 'The Enlightenment', were various. In the face of such a barrage upon the Christian Faith, there were three paths of retreat. The first was that taken by the Church of England into the secluded areas of 'Latitudinarianism', a viewpoint that may be described as 'broad convictions held with little emotion'. The Established Church became a haven for a quiet, unemotional theology, where orthodoxy was maintained as far as this was consistent with 'reason'. Horton Davies says that 'It was left to the Latitudinarians to conceive of a contradiction—Christianity without tears!' While there were some worthy churchmen who attempted to combat the advancing infidelity of the age, they could hardly be called heroes of the faith. Their tactics were exclusively intellectual rather than spiritual—a masterly use of words without the unction of the Holy Spirit.

Another escape route was taken by those Dissenters who were not too worried about capitulating to the enemy; they sacrificed much orthodoxy in order to appear rational, which meant a rejection of the evangelical Calvinism of the Puritans, a declension that became Arminianism and finally Unitarianism. Many Presbyterians became Unitarians in the eighteenth century. Albeit at a late stage in our period, Joshua Toulmin (1740–1815) was a notorious example: he lapsed from Presbyterian via Baptist to Unitarian convictions. Despite the heavy artillery of the Westminster Confession of Faith, the gunners deserted their positions. The Presbyterian strategy of men like Manton, Watson and Flavel did not convince the junior officers of a later generation.

The third path of retreat was that made by those who claimed to be faithful to the Calvinism of the Puritans. The spectacle was a sad one indeed; men who had formerly been the crack troops of Puritan Independency under Owen and Goodwin, retreated with Bibles in their hands, but with a weighty system of hyper-calvinism upon their backs. These stalwarts fled to the barren wastes of dead orthodoxy, where the watchword became 'survival'. The Independents were joined by the Particular Baptists, and they both agreed in this, that it was safest to rest their weary legs and take off their boots. Thus the liberalism of the Presbyterians and the ultra-orthodoxy of the Particular Baptists represented the early eighteenth-century extremes of traditional Calvinistic Dissent.

So, the general picture was far from encouraging. The Church of England appeared like a senile old man, still revealing traces of his former glory,

---

4   *God's Concern for His Glory in the British Isles* and *The Security of Christ's Church from the Gates of Hell* (London: John Clark, 1715), 50.

but now quite impotent. The Presbyterians suggest the picture of a once respectable young lady now despising the virtues of orthodoxy, a courtship which issued in the bastard of heterodoxy, while the Independents and Particular Baptists remind one of a prudish old couple with stern, joyless countenances, denouncing all this theological permissiveness with pharisaical precision. For the common people, this apparent defeat for the Christian faith only provided an excuse to live without regard for right or wrong, salvation or damnation, heaven or hell. This was an age that required a man of God who could provide an anchor during a storm of uncertainty and confusion. This was the age in which Almighty God called Edmund Calamy to serve Him and His people. But before we look at his ministry, let us take a brief look at the man.

CALAMY'S LINEAGE

We dare not ignore Edmund Calamy's remarkable ancestry. He was the third Edmund in a line beginning with his grandfather (1600–66) whose own Norman French Huguenot father came to England via Guernsey following the St Bartholomew persecution of 1572. A graduate of Pembroke Hall, Cambridge and an eminent preacher among the Puritans, Edmund I played a prominent part in the Westminster Assembly (1643–9). Our Edmund's father—Edmund II (1634–85)—was born in Bury St Edmunds, Suffolk, his father having previously ministered in Swaffham, Norfolk. Edmund II became Rector of Moreton in Essex, losing his living—as did his father in London—at the time of the Great Ejection (1662). In these momentous times—the Plague of 1665 followed by the Great Fire of London in 1666—Edmund I died. The sight of the devastated city soon brought him to his grave. Our Edmund was born in London in 1671. Then Edmund III's son Edmund IV (1697–1755) also became a minister of the Gospel. Not forgetting Calamy's significant Huguenot origins, he was conscious of his godly pedigree: 'I count it my honour to be descended on ye side both of Father & Mother from the Old Puritans'.[5] Accordingly, his early published sermons indicated that the author was 'E. F. & N.'—Edmundus Filius et Nepos (i.e. Edmund, son and grandson).

CALAMY'S LIFE

Knowing the grace of God early in his life, Edmund's education prepared him for future pastoral service. Robert Tatnal's school in Westminster, then Thomas Doolittle's Academy at Islington led via Thomas Walton's School in Bethnal Green to Merchant Taylors' School after his father's death in 1685. A year later he entered Samuel Cradock's Academy at Wickhambrook near Newmarket, Suffolk. Professing personal conversion at this time, he then

---

5   Cited by Wykes, Oxford DNB (2004).

'went to the Lord's Table'. In every respect, he declared: 'I must freely own I can look back on the time spent at Mr Cradock's academy with comfort and pleasure, blessing God for the benefit I there received … it was no small encouragement to me, to have this good old gentleman, upon his hearing me preach, a good many years after, come and embrace me in his arms, thanking God for the hand he had in my education'.[6]

In 1688, on the advice of the eminent Puritan John Howe (1630–1705), Edmund travelled to the Netherlands with other ministerial students to study at Utrecht. Studying in foreign Reformed institutions was the only way to obtain a higher education, entry to Oxford and Cambridge then being only open to Anglicans. This was a critical year for the future of European Protestantism. In October, Calamy saw William of Orange embark on his enterprise to liberate England from the Catholic designs of James II.

As much as Calamy and his generation valued the rigours of academic training, they were aware of the danger of unsanctified intelligence. Just as Baxter, Howe and others were careful to promote piety as well as sound learning, young Calamy shared their concerns. Besides escaping from a near-fatal accident on Dutch ice, he was aware of the threat of frozen orthodoxy. On leaving Holland for home in 1691, he expressed regret that though there were many English ministerial students at Utrecht,

> … we had no meetings among ourselves for prayer and Christian converse. Had I not been provided with many good practical books of English divinity, which I read frequently with profit and pleasure, I doubt it would have been worse with me than it was. From my own experience I can heartily recommend all students of theology, while laying in a stock of divinity in speculative way, to read pious and devotional works, so as to have a warmer sense of the things of God on their minds and hearts.[7]

Calamy's concern probably explains why he appreciated worshipping among the Huguenot refugees:

> In the French Church at Utrecht … there was … M. Saurin … a very grave man, and one of great depth of thought; who was for going to the bottom of a subject, and when he had doctrinally opened it, had a marvellous way of touching the passions.[8]

Returning to London, Edmund met the aged Richard Baxter. This was an important event in his life, as he makes clear:

6   *An Historical Account of My Own Life* (London: Henry Colburn and Richard Bentley, 1830), i. 145 (cited in A. H. Drysdale, 'Dr Edmund Calamy' in *Short Biographies for the People by Various Writers* (London: Religious Tract society, 1890), vii. No. 77, 6).

7   Ibid. 188 (Drysdale, 7).

8   *Account of My Own Life,* i. 145.

I particularly waited on Mr Baxter, who talked freely with me about my good old grandfather, for whom he declared a particular esteem.

Part of this esteem would have related to the 'Amyraldian' (or Davenantian!) convictions articulated by Edmund Calamy I during the sessions of the Westminster Assembly.[9] Edmund continued:

I several times heard [Mr Baxter] preach, which remembered not to have done before. He talked in the pulpit with great freedom about another world, like one that had been there, and was come as a sort of an express from thence to make a report concerning it. He was well advanced in years, but delivered himself in public, as well as in private, with great vivacity and freedom, and his thoughts had a peculiar edge. I told him of my design of going to Oxford, and staying sometime there, in which he encouraged me: and towards the end of the year, (Dec. 8) when I was actually there, he died; so that I should never have had an opportunity of seeing, hearing, or conversing with him, had I not done it now.[10]

The chief purpose of Calamy's studies at this time was to settle the question: was he to serve in the Church of England or among the Protestant Dissenters? So, aided by a letter of recommendation from one of his Dutch professors, he availed himself of the facilities of the Bodleian Library, Oxford. Among other works, he read Richard Hooker's *The Laws of Ecclesiastical Polity* (1590). However, as his detailed and comprehensive critique makes clear, Calamy remained totally unimpressed by the author's case for classical Anglicanism.[11] Carefully studying his Bible, 'and particularly the New Testament', he concluded that 'the plain worship of the Dissenters' was 'more agreeable to that, than the pompous way of the Church of England.'[12] William Chillingworth's *The Religion of Protestants* (1638) persuaded him that the Bible alone, rather than man-made confessions of faith (however sound), must be the basis of faith and concord among Christians.[13] Lodging with the Oxford Presbyterian minister Joshua Oldfield, Calamy was encouraged to preach his first sermon. As yet unordained, he felt somewhat intimidated by the event. His hearers included a 'greater number of scholars than usual'. However, our young preacher says "I bless God, however, I was not dashed, but came off pretty well. I discoursed both parts of the day from Heb. 2: 3, 'How shall we escape if we neglect so great salvation?'" Speaking of 'the great salvation of the Gospel', he expounded 'the necessity' of 'the satisfaction that

---

9   See Alan C. Clifford, *Atonement and Justification: English Evangelical Theology 1640–1790—An Evaluation* (Oxford: Clarendon Press, 1990/2002), 75.

10   Calamy, *An Historical Account*, i. 220–1.

11   Ibid. 235–46.

12   Ibid. 224–5.

13   Ibid. 227–34.

our blessed Saviour made for sin by offering up himself as a sacrifice ... according to the common way of our Protestant writers'.[14]

Returning to London in 1692, Calamy accepted a call from Matthew Sylvester's congregation at Meeting-House Court, Blackfriars. He and five other candidates were eventually ordained at Dr Samuel Annesley's Meeting House on 22 June 1694, Dr Daniel Williams—the eminent Presbyterian leader—and five ejected ministers officiating. This was the first public ordination of the Dissenters since the Act of Uniformity (1662). Calamy's first published sermon appeared around this time: *A Practical Discourse concerning Vows: with a special reference to Baptism and the Lord's Supper* (1694). This work, indicates Drysdale, 'proved' a blessing to 'more than his hearers. "If ever any saving impressions have been made upon my soul," writes one, "the reading of your treatise on vows was the great instrument. May I never forget the strong and lively influence it had on me."'[15]

The following year, Edmund Calamy became assistant to Dr Daniel Williams at Hand Alley, Bishopsgate Street.. In the same year (1695) he married Mary Watts, a marriage that proved happy and fruitful until Mary died in 1713. Their eldest son, Edmund IV (d. 1755) was born in 1698.

CALAMY'S LEGACY

Having recently commenced a regular and dedicated pastoral ministry in London lasting 38 years, Calamy also embarked on his career as an historian. So, in 1696, he aided Matthew Sylvester in publishing Richard Baxter's *Autobiography: the Reliquiae Baxterianae.* Thereafter, he amazingly found time to preserve and promote the memory of Baxter and the ejected ministers. Believing that Sylvester's devoted yet defective work would be more effective in an edited form, Calamy published *An Abridgement of Mr Baxter's History of His Life and Times with An account of the Ministers ... who were Ejected after the Restoration of King Charles II* (1702). Integral with his ministry, Calamy clearly felt called of God to transmit the heroic faith of Baxter and his brethren: "To let the Memory of these Men Dye is injurious to Posterity".[16] His *Abridgement* involved great courage, and it provoked a storm. At a time of continuing Anglican-inspired hostility to the heirs of the Puritans, this inspiring material marked out Edmund Calamy as 'the Champion of Nonconformity'.[17]

In 1702, Calamy was chosen as one of the Tuesday lecturers at Salters' Hall. Dating from earlier times, these public merchants lectures played a vital role in promoting Christian edification. Calamy's first and highly-impressive contribution was *Divine Mercy Exalted: or Free Grace in its Glory.*

---

14   Ibid. 268.

15   Drysdale, 11.

16   Wykes, op. cit.

17   Ibid.

Divine Mercy Exalted :

O R,

𝕱𝖗𝖊𝖊 𝕲𝖗𝖆𝖈𝖊

In its GLORY.

BEING A

SERMON

O N

ROM. IX. xvi.

Preach'd at the

Merchants Lecture

A T

Salters-Hall.

On Tuefday *Octob.* 20. 1702.

By *E. Calamy* E. F. & N.--

𝕻𝖚𝖇𝖑𝖎𝖘𝖍𝖊𝖉 𝖆𝖙 𝖙𝖍𝖊 𝕽𝖊𝖖𝖚𝖊𝖘𝖙 𝖔𝖋 𝕸𝖆𝖓𝖞
𝕰𝖓𝖈𝖔𝖚𝖗𝖆𝖌𝖊𝖗𝖘 𝖔𝖋 𝖙𝖍𝖊 𝕷𝖊𝖈𝖙𝖚𝖗𝖊.

London, Printed for *Tho. Parkhurft* at the Bible and
3 Crowns in *Cheapfide* ; *J. Robinfon* at the Golden
Lion in St: *Pauls Church-yard,* and *J. Lawrence* at
the Angel in the *Poultry,* 1703.

It was 'Published at the Request of Many Encouragers of the Lecture' the following year. Being the chief focus of this publication, the significance and importance of this lecture will shortly be explored.

That same year, Calamy became the minister of Tothill Street, Westminster. As his influence in the public affairs of the Dissenters began to increase, he was concerned clearly to define the Dissenting Presbyterian position vis-à-vis the Anglican Establishment, but without rancour and extremism. Thus, in the manner of Calvin, the Westminster divines and Baxter, and to vindicate the ejected clergy, this English churchman preached and published his *Defence of Moderate Nonconformity* (in three parts, 1703–5). For all his 'moderation', he presents a cogent and comprehensive biblical demonstration 'that presbyters are by Divine Right the same as Bishops'[18] and that the apostolic meaning of 'bishop' is *not* 'the sense the Church of England gives that word'.[19] Far from ignoring that biblical pastoral order is designed to promote practical piety in the lives of God's people, Calamy published Richard Baxter's *Practical Works* in 1707.[20] This was a major publishing event where Calamy was concerned. In his preface, after highlighting the 'valuable treatises of practical divinity published in this country', Calamy states that 'there are no writings of that kind among us, that have more of a true Christian spirit, a greater mixture of judgement and affection, or a greater tendency to revive pure and undefiled religion that have been more esteemed abroad, or more blessed at home for the awakening the secure, instructing the ignorant, confirming the wavering, comforting the dejected, recovering the profane, or improving such as are truly serious, than the Practical Works of this author'.[21] Adept at citing 'opposition' support, Calamy says 'That great man Bishop Wilkins was used to say of Mr Baxter, that if he had lived in the Primitive times he had been One of the Fathers of the Church: what then more fit than a collection of his works, that posterity may be taught to do him justice?[22]

Concerned as he was to promote vital and fervent piety, Calamy was aware of the danger of fanaticism. This became an issue with the arrival of certain 'French prophets' in London. Such had provided much of the inspiration in the Cevénnes region of France during the war of the Camisards (1702–10). These wild 'charismatic prophets' attracted a significant fringe following in this country, even influencing a member of Calamy's own congregation. Thus early in 1708 he preached and published two sermons entitled *A Caveat*

---

18   *Defence of Moderate Nonconformity* (London: Thomas Parkhurst, 1703), 71.

19   Ibid. 72.

20   *The Practical Works of the Late Reverend and Pious Mr Richard Baxter*, in Four Volumes (London: Thomas Parkhurst, 1707).

21   Ibid. p. iii.

22   Ibid.

against the New Prophets.[23] These very valuable sermons—appreciated by Queen Anne, no less—included a historical survey of fanaticism. Tracing its rise to the second-century 'impostor' Montanus, Calamy includes Roman Catholicism and Islam when he argues that 'the superstitious and idolatrous corruptions of the Church of Rome prevailed in the West, much about the same time as the Muhammadan fooleries spread far and near in the East. And in the Romish Church an enthusiastical spirit has remarkably prevailed ever since its first degeneracy. The histories of the lives of their saints are full of visions, extraordinary revelations and ecstasies. Whenever anything was to be undertaken for the advancement of the Church; and when any new doctrine or worship was to be established, a revelation has still been coined to direct it, and confirm it. Thus was the way paved for the settlement of image worship'.[24]

Concurrent with these concerns, Calamy preached an excellent series of sermons at Salters' Hall on *The Inspiration of the Old and New Testament* between 1704–6. Published in 1710, the author was anxious to rescue the Bible from any aspersions that might be cast on its Holy Spirit-inspired character. In his dedication to the Queen, in view of the recent fanatical disturbances, Calamy writes that 'Your gracious acceptance of my endeavours in opposition to a late pretended inspiration, has encouraged me with all humility to present to Your Majesty this defence of the ancient, but real inspiration of the Holy Writings of the Old and New Testament; which are the standard of our religion, and the foundation both of its certainty and authority'.[25]

This interesting dedication to the 'Chief support of the Reformed Interest' takes note of the recent military victories of Sir John Churchill, Duke of Marlborough (Blenheim, 1704; Ramillies, 1706; Oudenarde, 1708 and Malplaquet, 1709), the humbling of Louis XIV and the Act of Union:

> Your Majesty's reign will be celebrated in future for the steadiness of your counsels, and the glorious success of your Arms; for giving an effectual check to the aspiring designs of universal monarchy, and fixing the balance of Europe; for uniting your two British Kingdoms, and confirming your subjects of all persuasions, in a just esteem of the great blessing of MODERATION'.[26]

The year before these important sermons were published revealed Calamy's continuing concern with 'moderation'. Having witnessed first-hand in his youth the cruelties of religious persecution, he agreed with Baxter that both sides had been guilty during the Civil War. There had been

---

23   *A Caveat Against the New Prophets* (London: Thomas Parkhurst, 1708).

24   Ibid. 42.

25   *The Inspiration of the Holy Writings of the Old and New Testament Considered and Improved* (London: Thomas Parkhurst, 1710), The Dedication.

26   Ibid.

THE
INSPIRATION
OF THE
Holy Writings
OF THE
OLD and NEW TESTAMENT
Confider'd and Improv'd.

In FOURTEEN SERMONS preach'd at the
Merchants Lecture at *Salters Hall.*

By *EDMUND CALAMY*, D.D.

To which is added a Single SERMON
in Vindication of the *Divine Inſtitution*
of the Office of the MINISTRY,
preach'd at the fame Lecture.

LONDON:
Printed for *T. Parkhurſt* at the Bible and 3
Crowns in *Cheapſide* ; *J. Robinſon* at the Gol-
den Lion in St. *Paul's* Church-yard ; and
J. Lawrence at the Angel in the *Poultry* ; alſo
ſold by *J. Fox* in *Weſtminſter Hall.* 1710.

oppressive Presbyterians (not to forget the Cromwellian Independents) as well as oppressive Episcopalians. He thus sought to combine well-founded, sincerely-held convictions with a 'catholic spirit' or at least a respectful toleration of those who differ—not an easy balance to maintain. He therefore shunned the 'spirit of imposition'. During his travels to 'North Britain' in 1709, Calamy detected such a spirit during the General Assembly of the Church of Scotland, where he was an honoured guest, seated next to the Moderator. During one session when a suspected minister was being cross-examined, he caused some amusement when he remarked, "We in England should reckon this way of proceeding the inquisition revived."[27] Including a fellowship detour with Matthew Henry on the way home,[28]Calamy returned to London with more than an interesting glimpse of Scottish Presbyterianism. He was honoured with DDs from the Universities of Edinburgh, Aberdeen and Glasgow. Thus 'DD' replaced 'E. F. & N.' on the title pages of his books.

In the midst of all his pastoral, public and literary activities—a new edition of his *Account of the Ejected* appeared in 1713—Edmund Calamy knew personal sadness. His first wife, Mary died that year. Besides encouraging his brethren there, an extended preaching tour in the West of England allowed him to recover from his grief. However, he was troubled by the unhappy disturbances caused by advancing Unitarian ideas among some of the Dissenters in Exeter. A year later, his devoted mother died. Then, in the aftermath of the accession of Hanoverian Protestant King George I (1714–27), the first Jacobite rising indicated significant Roman Catholic opposition in the North of England and Scotland. To settle disturbed minds and hearts among loyal Protestants, Calamy preached and published three remarkable sermons in 1715 entitled *God's Concern for His Glory in the British Isles and The Security of Christ's Church from the Gates of Hell*.[29] These sermons include a masterly survey of the church history of the British Isles from the earliest times to the early eighteenth century, with suitable applications to assure believers that 'an Almighty Jesus has undertaken the conduct of His own Church, and engaged that it shall in the end be victorious over all the designs of its enemies'.[30] No less impressive than the scholarly erudition of our pastor-historian is the author's deeply-moving dedication to one grief-stricken 'Much Honoured the Lady Levet' who had cared for his mother in her last illness: 'Your Ladyship's constant tenderness' and 'endearing love

---

27   *An Historical Account*, ii.156.

28   See J. B. Williams, *Memoir … of the Rev. Matthew Henry* (1828; Edinburgh: The Banner of Truth Trust, rep. 1974), 100.

29   *God's Concern for His Glory in the British Isles and The Security of Christ's Church from the Gates of Hell* (London: John Clark, 1715).

30   Ibid. 87.

AN
ABRIDGEMENT
OF
Mr. Baxter's
HISTORY
OF HIS
LIFE and *TIMES*.

WITH

An Account of the Minifters, &c. who were Eje&ed after the Reftauration, of King *Charles* II.

Their Apology for themfelves, and their Adherents, containing the Grounds of their Nonconformity : Their Treatment in the Reign of King *Charles*, and King *James* ; and after the Revolution : And the continuation of their Hiftory, to the paffing of the Bill againft Occafional Conformity, in 1711.

The Second Edition: In Two VOLUMES. Vol. I.

By EDMUND CALAMY, *D. D.*

LONDON:

Printed for *John Lawrence*, at the *Angel* in the *Poultry* ; *J. Nicholfon*, and *J.* and *B. Sprint* in *Little-Britain* ; *R. Robinfon* in St. *Paul's* Church-yard, and *N. Cliffe*, and *D. Jackfon* in *Cheapfide*. 1713.

GOD's *Concern for his Glory in the* BRITISH *Ifles*;

AND

The Security of CHRIST'*s Church from the Gates of* Hell:

IN THREE

SERMONS

AT THE

MERCHANTS LECTURE

IN

SALTERS - HALL.

By EDMUND CALAMY, D.D.

LONDON:

Printed for JOHN CLARK, *at the* Bible *and* Crown, *in* Cheapfide *near the* Poultrey. 1715.

accompanied her to the last hours of her life'. This remarkable lady had not only stood out against the prevailing immorality of high society 'in one of the most populous and flourishing cities in the Universe'.[31] She had also suffered a degree of social rejection on account of her Dissenting convictions. She was clearly a trophy of God's grace in Dr Calamy's ministry. She died at Bath in 1722.[32]

In 1716, Calamy married Mary Jones who proved an ideal helpmeet for God's servant. His responsibilities increased when, on the death of Dr Daniel Williams that same year, Calamy became the recognised leader among the Dissenters, often acting on behalf of the three denominations, Presbyterian, Congregational and Baptist. Young men often sought his counsel respecting their ministerial aspirations. One such in 1718 was sixteen-year old Philip Doddridge. 'The Doctor' was not that impressed, urging young Philip to pursue a law career. As if to indicate that godly men are not infallible, happily for others and ourselves, God's call to Philip Doddridge was too clear to be discouraged. The rest is history.[33]

As Calamy's autobiography makes very clear, the descendants of the Puritans had largely lost the spiritual zeal of their forebears. That power for righteousness and godliness that had been so positively displayed in earlier times was now assuming a more negative character. This fact is clearly confirmed in the theological debates that dominated the life of the Dissenting congregations around the year 1719.

Theological decline chiefly began to make itself felt following the publication of works by such men as Emlyn, Clarke and Whiston. These men rejected the orthodox understanding of the Trinity, expounding views that eventually issued in Unitarianism. The new liberal ideas of the age revived the ancient heresy of Arianism. In no place did Arianism obtain a firmer grip than among the Presbyterian congregations at Exeter which favoured the heterodox James Peirce. The managing committee of the churches in Exeter decided to refer the matter to the ministers of the London churches. A committee of the three main dissenting bodies—Presbyterian, Independent and Baptist—drew up a 'Paper of Advices' to be sent to Exeter, as a means of reconciling the contending parties. This document was discussed by an assembly of the London ministers at the famous Salters' Hall on February 19, 1719. A heated division of opinion soon followed between those advocating a more conciliatory position and those who argued for a strict prohibition of ministers advancing Arian views.

---

31   Ibid. dedication.

32   'Oct. 15. Died my good friend, the Lady Levet, at Bath' (*An Historical Account*, ii.463).

33   See my *The Good Doctor: Philip Doddridge of Northampton, a Tercentenary Tribute* (Norwich: Charenton Reformed Publishing, 2002).

The Salters' Hall Conference is a landmark in the history of English Nonconformity. From this time, the congregations became largely introspective, and mutual suspicion permeated the ranks of the ministers. The Conference revealed a sad anomaly, such that, recalling his study of Chillingworth's *The Religion of Protestants* at Oxford, Dr Calamy complained of 'a spirit of imposition'.[34] This development was not characteristic of the Dissenters. In 1662, these men had suffered because the Act of Uniformity had been imposed on them. How could they now yield to a spirit of persecuting imposition? On the other hand, many of the Presbyterians like those at Exeter, were now claiming further liberties in rejecting their own doctrinal standards. Over-heated logic tends to push things to extremes, and what was a desire for liberty *under* the Gospel in 1662 was becoming liberty *without* the Gospel in 1719. Orthodox liberty became heterodox liberalism.

A further development following Salters' Hall was that those of the 'Subscribing' party naturally tended to question the orthodoxy of the 'Nonsubscribers', even when there were no just grounds to do so. An inquisitorial attitude was at large. Those who advocated 'charity' in disputes were automatically suspected of Arianism, while those who contended for truth were accused of bigotry. There were many cases of both liberalism and bigotry, but there were others who sought to achieve a biblical balance. This division of opinion did not reflect any differences on the doctrines of the Trinity and the Deity of Christ, but simply whether human articles of faith should be subscribed to. As one minister present said, "It was not from any doubts in our minds as to the generally received opinions upon that subject, but from our scrupling to subscribe to any human articles of faith."[35] Despite the amount of heat dissipated, two sets of advice were sent down to Exeter. From all this, for all their distaste for Arianism, Dr Calamy and others remained uninvolved.

Together with the Congregational leader, Dr Isaac Watts (1674–1748)— undoubtedly more well-known on account of his hymns—Dr Edmund Calamy was probably the most distinguished example of this anti-imposition outlook. Others who attended the unsavoury debates agreed that Calamy and Watts took the wisest course in not attending. Certainly, if anyone doubted his attachment to truth, contrary to Dr Watts' later dubious deviations, Dr Calamy demonstrated his sound Bible-based convictions in his magnificent *Thirteen Sermons Concerning the Doctrine of the Trinity,* preached at Salters' Hall in 1719. When they were published in 1722, they included four other sermons from 1720 vindicating the genuineness of 'that celebrated Text, 1 John 5: 7'. Never perhaps has such sound, sanctified scholarship appeared in relatively-popular dress in the defence of the authentic biblical Gospel

---

34   See his narrative and assessment in *An Historical Account,* ii.403–29.
35   Thomas Wright, *The Life of Isaac Watts* (London: Farncombe & Sons, 1914), 139.

THIRTEEN
SERMONS

Concerning the Doctrine of the

TRINITY.

Preach'd at the

MERCHANT'S-LECTURE, at *Salter's-Hall.*

TOGETHER WITH

A VINDICATION of that Celebrated Text,
1 *John* v. 7. from being *Spurious;* and an Explication of it, upon the Suppofition of its being *Genuine* : In Four SERMONS, Preach'd at the fame
Lecture. *An.* 1719, 1720.

By EDMUND CALAMY, *D. D.*

*Quifqui hæc legit, ubi pariter certus eft, pergat mecum ; ubi
pariter hæfitat, quæres mecum : ubi errorem fuum cog-
nofcit, redeat ad me ubi meum, revocet me.* Auguftinus de Trinitate. Lib. I. cap. iii.
*Cum homines Deum quærant. & ad intelligentiam Trinita-
tis (pro captu infirmitatis humanæ) animum intendunt ;
facillime debent ignofcere errantibus in tanti pervefti-
gatione fecreti.* Auguftinus ibidem. Lib. II. cap. i.

L O N D O N:

Printed for JOHN CLARK, *at the* Bible *and*
Crown *in the* Poultry, *near* Cheapfide. 1722.

than in these sermons. In the hope that 'it might bring more persons to read the discourses',[36] they were dedicated by permission to King George I, to whom Dr Calamy had presented a loyal address in the name of the Protestant Dissenters in 1717.[37] There were, of course, perfectly valid political expectations in all this, as Calamy makes clear:

> I humbly presented my book to His Majesty, who received me very graciously, took it into his hands, and looked on it; and then was pleased to tell me, he took us Dissenters for his hearty friends, and desired me to let my brethren in the city know, that in the approaching election of members of Parliament, he depended on them, to use their utmost influence, wherever they had any interest, in favour of such as were hearty for him and his family.[38]

While the Dr Calamy and others had grave concerns about the spiritual health of the Dissenters at this time, his own ministry knew the unmistakeable blessing of God. A growing congregation required a new building, as he joyfully explains:

> April 23. 1721 I entered on the new place of worship, erected at a considerable expense in Long Ditch, Westminster [in Princes Street]. It was near two years building. Soon after, the whole was paid for, which I thought I had reason to reckon among the considerable mercies of my life. The necessity we were under of erecting a new place of worship was great, and the difficulties we met with were very considerable; but we had our helps, the juncture was favourable, and a kind Providence carried us through all ... To God be the praise!'[39]

Regarding the 'living church' that filled the building, one observer wrote:

> [Dr Calamy] had many persons of considerable figure in his congregation, and continued to preach there till his death, discharging the duties of the Christian ministry with great constancy and diligence.[40]

By all accounts, if he seldom rose to the heights of Baxterian eloquence, Dr Calamy was a good, solid, warm and faithful preacher.[41] His large congregation obviously appreciated his pastoral emphases. His published sermons reveal a minister with the highest spiritual concerns. Promoting—as

---

36   See *An Historical Account*, ii. 444.

37   Ibid. ii. 366ff.

38   Ibid. 446–7.

39   Ibid. 441–2.

40   Cited in John Stoughton, *Religion in England under Queen Anne and the Georges 1702–1800* (London: Hodder and Stoughton, 1878), i. 185.

41   A visitor from Northampton (and clearly no friend of Presbyterianism) remarked on Calamy: 'He is a good preacher, but a zealous man for the Kirk, ...' (cited in Stoughton, *Religion in England*, i. 226). Another observed that 'He preached very well, but he has a stiff, affecting manner of delivery, though a good voice and the delivery pretty good' (*The Diary of Dudley Ryder, 1715–1716*, ed. W. Matthews (1939), 224, cited in Wykes, Oxford DNB).

did Richard Baxter—'serious, practical Christianity' and discouraging 'party spirit' and censoriousness, he urged:

> Let it be your endeavour to get well furnished minds, warm hearts, governable spirits, tender consciences, and heavenly affections, and your stability and fruitfulness will be signal. Often reflect on the strength and sacredness of the divine vows you are under [especially regarding Baptism and the Lord's Supper], ...and take care to live faithfully up to them, if you have any regard to the favour of God, the honour of Christ, your own present peace, or future happiness.[42]

As a pastor's pastor (in a brotherly not a pseudo-episcopal sense!), Calamy's ordination sermons clearly set forth the biblical ministerial model. Regarding doctrine, a pastor should avoid a man-made confessionalism:

> Adhere firmly to [your doctrine] as it is delivered in the Holy Scriptures, which are the true standard which all creeds and confessions, systems and theological tracts and discourses are to be measured by: and be ready to maintain and defend it, and oppose them that teach any other doctrine.[43]

Regarding a pastor's personal piety, Calamy urges:

> Aim at excelling in that love to God, that zeal for Christ, that compassion for the souls of men, that humility of mind, that mastery of your appetites, and that mortification and deadness to this world, that becomes the character and profession you have taken upon you.[44]

Regarding a pastor's public example, they should aim at a holy consistency between lip and life:

> Men are so disposed, that they'll much more mind how you live, than what you say. And what can be more dreadful, than for ministers to pull down and destroy by their bad examples, what they seem to take pains to build up with the words of their mouths![45]

CALAMY'S LAST YEARS

Believing that posterity would be 'injured' without an awareness of its godly heritage, Calamy continued with his historical ministry. In 1724 he published the *Memoirs of John Howe*. Three years later—1727—he published *A continuation of the Account of the Ministers* (including further account of Baxter). Despite the national rejoicing at the accession of King George II that same year, Calamy's public involvement in presenting loyal addresses at Court on behalf of the

---

42 *A Practical Discourse concerning Vows: with a special reference to Baptism and the Lord's Supper* (London: Thomas Parkhurst, 1704), The Epistle Dedicatory.

43 *The Principles and Practice of Moderate Nonconformists with Respect to Ordination* (London: John Clark, 1717), 26.

44 Ibid. 28.

45 Ibid. 29.

Protestant Dissenters[46] and the magnificence of the Coronation (some of which he witnessed[47]), his heart was heavy. Many lapsed Dissenters were conforming to the Church of England and the health of the churches generally was not good. He longed for true spiritual revival:

> Let us beg a fresh effusion of the Divine Spirit from on high to revive the power and life of religion in our midst. Nothing can be more manifest than that the Church of Christ at this day is most sadly degenerated, has long been in a very languishing state, and is become too much like the rest of the world. Formality has eaten out the spirit of piety; and selfishness, covetousness, pride, wrathfulness, envy and malice have most shamefully abounded in the Christian Church, and sadly defaced, disquieted and infested it. And all parties have been such sharers in the common guilt that none must pretend an exemption. The great doctrines of the Christian religion have lost their force, and are professedly believed but for fashion's sake. ... And many that make great profession are lost in carnality and are crumbled into parties enflamed against each other, striving which shall get the better, which is much to be lamented.[48]

Calamy took note of widespread discussion in 1730 about 'the decay of the Dissenting interest'.[49] He read most of the pamphlets produced in response to *An Inquiry into the Causes of the Decay*, authored by a Dissenter who shortly after joined the Anglicans. Philip Doddridge's anonymous response[50] was noted, as is another by Isaac Watts.[51] In some respects he was puzzled by concern over numbers. In some areas growth was evident if decline occurred elsewhere. Certainly, his own congregation was flourishing, as were others in London. However, he did not deny that 'at the same time, a real decay of serious religion, both in the Church and out of it, was very visible'.[52]

Calamy's health began to decline by 1729. That summer he spent ten weeks at Scarborough 'taking the waters'. Yet his faith remained bright and his focus unchanged. In 1731 he preached at Dr Williams's Library to the ministers of the three denominations (the first of such gatherings) on *Gospel Ministers,*

---

46   *An Historical Account*, ii. 496–500.

47   'Wednesday, Oct. 11, the King and Queen were crowned, in great pomp and state. The procession to and from the Abbey upon that occasion, of which I was a spectator, was very magnificent. Dr Potter, Bishop of Oxford, preached the coronation sermon from 2 *Chron. ix. 8*' (ibid. ii. 500).

48   *A Continuation of the Account of the Ministers*, cited in Drysdale, 16.

49   See *An Historical Account*, ii. 529–31.

50   *Free Thoughts on the most probable means of reviving the Dissenting Interest* (London: Richard Hett, 1730).

51   *An Humble Attempt towards the Revival of Practical Religion among Christians, and particularly the Protestant Dissenters* (London: 1731).

52   *An Historical Account*, ii. 531.

the Salt of the Earth.[53] Planning another health visit to Bath in 1732 (though not expecting that his end was that close), Dr Calamy preached what proved to be his farewell sermon:

> Were I assured this was the last sermon I should ever preach to you, I know not any better text to fasten on than my text, 'The grace of our Lord Jesus Christ be with you all,' and to this I can heartily say Amen. For, brethren, my heart's desire and prayer for you is that you may be saved. And may you but have the grace of the Lord Jesus Christ with you, I shall not doubt of it. ... May it be on you and in you more and more. May you have it in your homes and in your attendance on God in His house. You will be much in my thoughts, and I trust I shall not be out of yours.[54]

Calamy returned to London where he died on 9 June. Daniel Mayo (Doddridge's former pastor at Kingston-upon-Thames) preached his funeral sermon. There we learn that:

> There was a constant calmness and easiness on his mind with respect to another world, a firm faith in the Gospel method of salvation, and good hope through grace. He was ever inclined to thankfulness, without distrust or complaint, and comforted several in distress that came to visit him. ... A few days before his death, he plainly apprehended that his end was near, and did in a particular manner pray for a blessing on his wife and children, that were about him, and then took his leave of them, and hardly ever had the use of his reason afterwards.[55]

We may surely say, 'The memory of the righteous is blessed' (*Proverbs 10: 7*).

Dr Calamy's unswerving faith that 'an Almighty Jesus has undertaken the conduct of His own Church, and engaged that it shall in the end be victorious over all the designs of its enemies' was soon to be demonstrated. In the year of his death, a young man from Gloucester named George Whitefield entered Pembroke College Oxford. His life-transforming evangelical conversion took place in 1735. As we are about to discover, a pioneer in the Methodist revival was the already-mentioned Dissenter Philip Doddridge, who was to meet and befriend the eloquent evangelist in 1739.

Dr Calamy was right. The rest is history, glorious history! He was right too about Dissent: the old Anglican wineskin could not contain the new wine of Methodism. The Wesleyans eventually joined the Dissenters in 1795, followed by the Welsh Calvinistic Methodists in 1811.[56] This is not to ignore the Evangelical movement in the Church of England. Yet despite the

---

53   This was never published and remains in MS at DWL (and is yet to be read by myself).

54   Cited in Drysdale, 16.

55   Cited in *An Historical Account*, ii. 535.

56   Michael R. Watts, *The Dissenters* (Oxford: The Clarendon Press, 1978), 449.

later influence of John Newton and the staunchly-anti-Anglo-Catholic first Bishop of Liverpool J. C. Ryle, even 20th century Anglican Evangelicalism was to fall victim to the culture of compromise embedded in the Church of England since Tudor times. Rome-ward drift was to become evident in the ecumenical sympathies of John Stott and J. I. Packer, the former also making alarming concessions in a liberal direction.[57] Sadly, enhanced by 'experience-before-doctrine' charismanic confusion (about which Calamy would have something to say from his encounters with the 'French prophets'),[58] this shared liberal ecumenism was to have a devastating impact on Nonconformity during the same period. In the 21st century, a return to Edmund Calamy's robust Luther-like biblical Protestantism remains the only antidote to these deplorable developments:

If the Scriptures are divinely inspired, the whole foundation of the Popish religion is rotten. Our [Protestant] religion is bottomed upon the Scriptures, which having been given by inspiration of God, cannot deceive us. The Scriptures, which came from God, and were drawn up under His conduct and influence, as a directory to His Church and People in all ages, are with us a thousand times more venerable, and unspeakably more sacred, and of greater authority, than the doctrines, or sentiments of any creatures whatsoever.

One little sentence of those divine books; that sentence in particular which declares, that *God so loved the world, that he gave his only begotten Son, that whosoever believeth in him might not perish, but have everlasting life* [John 3:16], with us deserves incomparably more respect and regard, than all the definitions or determinations, resolutions or decrees, of princes or doctors, popes or councils, men or angels.

We keep so close to those Scriptures, being satisfied of their heavenly original, that our pastors and teachers can safely join in with the great Apostle, and say, *Though we, or an angel from heaven, preach any other Gospel unto you, than that which we have preached unto you, let him be accursed* [Galatians 1:8]. And this is our glory. Herein lies the peculiar firmness of our religion, and that which distinguishes it from all others, that it came entirely from those Scriptures that were divinely inspired.[59]

THE CALAMY LINK

We conclude our biographical survey with a significant and interesting aspect of Edmund Calamy's legacy. This concerns that young man whom he mistakenly

---

57   See Iain H. Murray, *Evangelicalism Divided* (Edinburgh: The Banner of Truth Trust, 2000), 112ff.

58   See *A Caveat Against the New Prophets* (London: Thomas Parkhurst, 1708).

59   *The Inspiration of the Holy Writings of the Old and New* Testament (London: T. Parkhurst, 1710), 313–15.

discouraged from entering the Christian ministry, Philip Doddridge. In his early days at Kibworth in Leicestershire, young pastor Philip received a gift of books (from a Mr Haldon) which had a dramatic impact on his development and future ministry. These were Dr Calamy's 4-volume 1707 edition of the *Practical Works of Richard Baxter*. Unimpressed by the works of those 'mysterious men', the over-orthodox John Owen and Thomas Goodwin, Doddridge had been drawn to the writings of Archbishop John Tillotson. However, in 1724, Calamy's *Baxter* changed everything. Writing to his brother-in-law, Doddridge revealed the Apostle of Kidderminster's impact upon him:

> Baxter is my particular favourite, and it is impossible to tell you how much I am charmed with the devotion, good sense, and pathos, which are everywhere to be found in that writer. I cannot indeed forbear looking upon him as one of the greatest orators that our nation ever produced, ... I have lately been reading his *Gildas Salvianus* [The Reformed Pastor], which has cut me out some work among my people, that will take me off from so close an application to my private studies as I would otherwise covet.[60]

Whether or not Dr Calamy ever knew about this, his influence in Doddridge's development would have delighted him. He would doubtless have been astonished to know that after his death in 1732, his Princes Street, Westminster congregation desired Philip Doddridge as Calamy's successor! During a visit to London in July, 1733, Philip wrote to his wife Mercy, "I have been strongly besieged by Dr Calamy's people."[61] However, Doddridge—who in the same letter also refers to a financial inducement to join the Anglicans—had no doubt that God had called him to serve as a Protestant Dissenter in Northampton.

Despite that early discouragement, Doddridge clearly came to admire Calamy's contribution. Over twenty years later, the Northampton pastor cited Calamy's views on church order in his *Family Expositor*. Commenting on Acts 20: 25–8 (where Paul calls all the Ephesian elders 'overseers' or 'bishops'), Doddridge remarked:

> The late learned, moderate and pious Dr Edmund Calamy observes, that, if the apostles had been used (as some assert) to ordain diocesan bishops in their last visitation, this had been a proper time to do it; or that, if Timothy had been already ordained bishop of Ephesus, Paul, instead of calling them all bishops, would have surely given some hint to enforce Timothy's authority among them,

---

60   See my *The Good Doctor: Philip Doddridge of Northampton*, 36.

61   Geoffrey F. Nuttall (ed.), *Calendar of the Correspondence of Philip Doddridge DD* (1702–1751), Letter 385.

especially considering what is added, ver. 29, 30 (see Dr Calamy's *Defence*, Vol. 1, p. 78).[62]

A final example of the Calamy-Doddridge link concerns revival. As we have seen, the London minister longed and prayed for 'a fresh effusion of the Divine Spirit from on high to revive the power and life of religion in our midst'. Little did he know that it was commencing while he was praying. Indeed, something remarkable happened at Northampton in 1729. In that year, soon after Doddridge's settlement at Castle Hill, he preached his sermon *Christ's Invitation to Thirsty Souls*. The preacher wrote of the occasion that 'something of a peculiar blessing seemed to attend the discourse, when delivered from the pulpit; and that to such a degree, as I do not know to have been equalled by any other sermon I ever preached'.[63] This was six years before Whitefield's conversion (1735) and nine before John Wesley's (1738)! This extraordinary sermon was eventually published in 1748, some years after the revival had become a nationwide phenomenon. When Whitefield obtained and read a copy, he wrote to Doddridge:

> ... dear Sir, I must thank you for your sermon. It contains the very life of preaching, I mean sweet invitations to close with Christ. I do not wonder you are dubbed a Methodist on account of it ...[64]

Recalling the unhappy division within the Methodist movement over Calvinism and Arminianism, is it too much to suggest that—by the grace of God—the revival began, not through the Owenite Whitefield or the Arminian Wesley but the Baxterian Philip Doddridge? Professor Alan Everitt expressed the opinion that 'If any event can be regarded as beginning the Evangelical Movement it is probably the appointment of the Independent Philip Doddridge to Castle Hill Chapel in 1729'.[65]

A further comment is in order. As we will shortly see, in the light of Calamy's 1703 sermon *Divine mercy Exalted*, one easily detects a distinct 'Calamynian' orthodoxy in Doddridge's *Christ's Invitation to Thirsty Souls*, delivered as it was with something close to Baxterian fervour.[66] In which

---

62   See Doddridge's *Works* (Leeds: E. Williams & E. Parsons, 1805), viii. 209. Doddridge cites Calamy's *Defence of Moderate Nonconformity* (London: Thomas Parkhurst, 1703).

63   *The Good Doctor*, 172–3.

64   Ibid. 172.

65   Ibid. 173.

66   For a recent discussion of Doddridge's theology, see Richard A. Muller, 'Philip Doddridge and the Formulation of Calvinistic Theology in an Era of Rationalism and Deconfessionalization' in R. D. Cornwall and W. Gibson (eds.), *Religion, Politics and Dissent, 1660–1832* (Aldershot: Ashgate, 2010), 65–84. While he recognises the Baxter-Doddridge link, Dr Muller's attempt to distance Doddridge from Amyraut's type of hypothetical conditionalism is unfounded (see Doddridge, *Works*, v. 240; x. 327).

case, sharing, transmitting and mediating the same spiritual ethos, Edmund Calamy made a distinct contribution to the great work of God known as the Evangelical Awakening of the eighteenth century. Doddridge thus declared:

In the history of the Evangelists …we there find our blessed Redeemer publishing the free and unlimited offers of his grace, to all that were willing to accept it… Do you thirst for the pardon of sin? … Do you thirst for the favour of God? … Do you thirst for the communications of the Spirit? The Lord Jesus Christ can abundantly relieve you … Do you thirst for the joys and glories of the heavenly world? The Lord Jesus Christ is able to relieve you … I know there is a great deal of difference between the common operations of the Spirit on the minds of those who continue obstinate and impenitent, and those special influences by which he sweetly but powerfully subdues the hearts of those who are chosen in Christ Jesus before the foundation of the world. Yet I am persuaded, that none to whom the Gospel comes are utterly neglected by that sacred agent … Behold then the tears of a Redeemer over perishing souls, and judge by them of the compassions of His heart … Surely nothing can be more melting, than such tears, falling from such eyes, and in such circumstances. And if our Lord could not give up the impenitent sinners of Jerusalem without weeping over them, surely He will not despise the humble and penitent soul, who is, perhaps with tears, seeking His favour, and flying to his grace as his only refuge …

The tears of our blessed Redeemer must needs be convincing and affecting, if the mind be not sunk into an almost incredible stupidity; but his blood is still more so. View him, my brethren, not only in the previous scenes of his abasement, his descent from heaven, and his abode on earth; but view him on mount Calvary, extended on the cross, torn with thorns, wounded with nails, pierced with a spear; and then say, whether there be not a voice in each of these sacred wounds, which loudly proclaims the tenderness of his heart, and demonstrates, beyond all possibility of dispute or suspicion, his readiness to relieve the distressed soul, that cries to him for the blessings of the gospel. He died to purchase them, not for himself, but for us; and can it be thought he will be unwilling to bestow them? We may well conclude that he loved us, since he shed his blood to wash us from our sins (Rev. 1: 5): … that while we were strangers and enemies he hath died for us. (Rom. 5: 8).

I hope, through grace, there are some such among you … who are now thirsting for the blessings of the Gospel … To you my friends, I would briefly say … Go directly, and plead the case with Him … for that soul will surely be relieved, and God in Christ be glorified and exalted.[67]

Having sampled Philip Doddridge's sermon, let us learn and profit from these things. May God have mercy upon our desperately needy world, to His eternal glory. Amen!

---

67   *The Good Doctor,* 171–2.

Until his early death in 1751, Doddridge became personally involved in the Methodist movement. Besides making his own unique contribution to the Great Awakening, he served as an occasional adviser to Whitefield and John Wesley. But the Dissenters remained his closest friends, and, to cap it all, during his various visits to London, he often enjoyed lunch and fellowship with Edmund Calamy IV.[68] They doubtless discussed often the enduring legacy of Dr Edmund Calamy, the 'Champion of Nonconformity'!

CALAMY'S LECTURE

Turning lastly to a significant and important publication, in a thoroughly dismissive manner, the Unitarian historian Alexander Gordon declared that 'no one reads Calamy's sermons'.[69] Neither does he bother to mention the important Salters' Hall lecture *Divine Mercy Exalted: or Free Grace in its Glory* (1703), to which we now turn. Even Dr David Wykes (also a Unitarian), while stating that 'Calamy was Baxterian in theology',[70] fails to mention this most important work wherein Calamy's Baxterian soteriology is evident. Far more sympathetically, Alexander Drysdale commends the sermon as 'entirely evangelical' even if it lacks 'the warmth and glow of utterance congenial to such a theme'.[71] But this 'sermonic lecture' was clearly intended not only to edify his hearers but to advertise the young minister's commitment to 'Baxterian Calvinism' *vis-à-vis* the prevailing extremes of Arminianism and Owenism. Judging by the title page, it met a widespread need for clarity over many of the most controversial issues of recent history. Indeed, this work is a well-structured, biblically-based and luminously-insightful exposition of the Gospel which repays careful study. The following inadequate overview is intended to indicate the main drift of Calamy's case.

In the preface to *Divine Mercy Exalted*, Calamy reveals his perspective on the subject in hand. In order to express his position, he appeals not to the over-refined orthodoxy of the Westminster Assembly (1643–9) but to the unexaggerated theology of the Synod of Dort (1618). While he often made respectful references to the WCF in later years, Calamy was evidently happier with the more moderate stances of Dort and of Bishop John Davenant who was one of the British delegates at the Synod:

> I have considered Divine grace as actually discovering itself to sinners, rather than as purposed in the Decree: but he that would see that discussed, and the doctrine of particular election maintained, consistently with a general love of God to the world, would do well to consult the learned and peaceable Bishop

---

68   See Doddridge, *Calendar,* Letters 436, 1082, 1337, 1337, 1377.

69   See the article on Calamy in the *DNB* (Oxford: OUP, 1885–1900).

70   David L. Wykes, 'Calamy, Edmund (1671–1732)', *Oxford Dictionary of National Biography* (Oxford University Press, 2004).

71   Drysdale, 'Dr Edmund Calamy', 11.

Davenant's *Animadversions upon Hoard's Treatise of God's Love to Mankind*; a book which is not valued according to its worth: though one would think it were therefore the more to be regarded in these points, because the worthy author was so considerable a member of the forementioned Synod, in which the controversy about grace and free-will was so distinctly debated.[72]

Without even a single reference to Richard Baxter, Calamy does what his hero also did—appeal to John Davenant's 'middle way' between 'free will' Arminianism and what became 'limited atonement' Owenism (and later hypercalvinist Gillism). In the context of these debates, Davenant's *Dissertation on the Death of Christ* is well known (even though the Banner of Truth Trust deleted it from their recent edition of Davenant's *Exposition of Colossians,* an omission remedied by Dr Digby James of the Quinta Press).[73] However, Calamy's citation of Davenant's lesser-known-work against the Arminian Anglican Samuel Hoard is important in dealing with the predestinarian background to the atoning work of Christ. Indeed, Davenant's *Animadversions* is probably the best, balanced albeit brief biblical exposition of predestination ever written. Besides resolving numerous knotty issues, it provides practical guidance to preachers on how and how not to preach on the subject. In the process of rescuing the Bible's teaching on this subject from Hoard's repeated misrepresentations, Davenant also rescues John Calvin from the unjust aspersions cast on him on account of the doctrine.[74] In short, Davenant's teaching was the perfect Bible-based antidote to a later extremism of the kind Baxter and later Calamy sought to oppose. This was a Gospel stance[75] which could not only claim support from Calvin and many other reformers. Above all, Calamy—like Baxter—believed such was the true teaching of the Holy Scriptures.

Calamy's text is 'So then it is not of him that willeth, nor of him that runneth, but of God that sheweth mercy' (*Romans 9: 16*). He has no

---

72   *Divine Mercy Exalted: or Free Grace in its Glory* (London: 1703), pp. iii–iv.

73   See my Introduction to John Davenant, *A Dissertation on the Death of Christ* (Weston Rhyn: Quinta Press, 2006).

74   See John Davenant, *Animadversions Upon a Treatise Intitled God's Love to Mankind* (Cambridge: 1641), 26, 39, 42, 64, 96, 99, 135, 139–43, etc.

75   'Christ died for all and every singular person, who by repentance and faith in His blood may, according to the tenor of the Gospel, have eternal life given him through Jesus Christ our Lord. And Christ died thus for all, not only because His death was in regard of the worth a sufficient ransom for all and more than all, but because it is God's settled purpose, by Christ's bloodshed to save any man that shall believe truly in Him, and to save no man that continueth an unbeliever. Christ died not to save any few selected ones without their repentance and faith; and Christ died not with an exception or exclusion of any one man in the world from the benefit of salvation, performing the condition of faith and repentance' (ibid. 472–3).

hesitation in affirming that 'the reason why the gentiles, and why particular sinners that are unworthy, are embraced and peculiarly favoured by God, while the Jews and other sinners are left in their chosen impenitency and infidelity, is not from any antecedent worthiness or disposedness, that God saw in the former above the latter, but from his free differencing grace and mercy'.[76] In short, salvation 'is not to be ultimately resolved into human pains and industry: the spring of it is to be searched for, not in man but in God'.[77] Indeed, God's mercy 'is exercised in a sovereign way'.[78]

Yet Calamy is quick to rescue the text from fatalistic hypercalvinist inertia when he says: 'Yet [the Apostle] is far from intimating that willing and running is needless; or that the mercy of God will act alone ... without a subservient agency on our part'.[79] Would we tell the farmer and the businessman that 'the blessing of the Lord that maketh rich' (*Prov. 10: 22*) does not require their 'diligence and industry'?[80] Developing his case from text after text, Calamy encourages (with a touch of Baxterian eloquence) the unassured seeker after God who desires but doubts God's mercy, thus:

> He that waits to be gracious, and hath assured us with an oath, that He hath 'no pleasure in the death of the wicked, but that he turn from his way and live' (*Ezek. 33: 11*); He that seeks us so carefully as lost sheep while we are wandering from Him in the ways of vanity and folly, cannot certainly turn His back upon us, when our wills are fixed for Him; and we are bent upon running in the way of His commandments.[81]

Tracing our salvation to God's mercy, Calamy carefully explains what his text is *not* saying. In the case of those who are unsaved, the cause is our sin and unwillingness, not 'God that delighteth in severity'.[82]

> The text keeps on the bright side, and states the case of those whom God treats and embraces as His own; and there it tells us we must fasten upon unaccountable mercy as the rise of all: but if we turn to the darker side, and view the case of those who are cast off by God, we are not allowed to fasten upon unaccountable severity as the procuring cause. ... Our saviour hath Himself sufficiently cleared that matter, when He in so many words tells those among whom He preached, and before whom He wrought His miracles, that this was their ruin: 'Ye will not come to me that ye might have life' (*Jn. 5: 40*).[83]

---

76   *Divine Mercy Exalted*, 5–6.

77   Ibid. 7.

78   Ibid. 9.

79   Ibid. 9–10.

80   Ibid. 10.

81   Ibid. 13.

82   Ibid. 14.

83   Ibid. 14–15.

After explaining that sinners are lost from their own 'self-hardening', and that Romans 9: 22–3 only speaks of '*prior* preparation' in the case of the saved, Calamy concludes—and the Greek supports him—that God 'with much long-suffering and patience endured [the unsaved]. A clear evidence that He rather permitted them when left to themselves, to harden their own hearts, than positively concurred in it. And indeed, though Divine mercy is ever free, yet God's severity is always deserved'.[84]

Having refuted common ultra-Calvinist abuse of the doctrine of predestination, Calamy then proceeds in his first main proposition to present Christ's coming into the world:

> The providing a Mediator, and all overtures about reconciliation through Him, are 'of God that sheweth mercy'. Nothing but meer pity and compassion could move Him, when so affronted, to think of a Saviour for a lost world; whom He might have left to perish in their miserable state.[85]

In his second proposition, Calamy highlights the 'given' unmerited nature of God's grace. Thus we should simply be amazed at the Gospel, realising that had God withheld His mercy from humanity, no injustice would have been done. After showing how 'providential means' and 'ministerial helps' in the recovery of sinners combine to 'point out their Saviour to them, set Him in all His charms before them, and press them to accept His offered help',[86] Calamy reminds us of God's sovereign initiative in dealing with nations:

> Some that pretend to have made an exact calculation, do observe, that if the earth, as far as it is at this day known, were divided into 30 equal parts, 19 of them are pagan, 6 Muhammadan, and but 5 Christian. Who that gives way to consideration, can forbear wondering that these five parts of the earth should be more favoured than the other 25![87]

In his third main proposition, Calamy is careful to show that when sinners seek God, their endeavours are 'not from themselves, but given and stirred up by God that sheweth mercy'.[88] In expounding our natural deadness and aversion regarding spiritual things from a range of biblical texts, Calamy is careful (in Amyraldian style) to distinguish between 'moral' and 'natural' impotency.[89] Indeed, 'dead' sinners are 'alive' and guilty with active hostility to God! It is our *wilful* opposition rather than any defect in psychological

---

84 Ibid. 16–17.
85 Ibid. 17.
86 Ibid. 21.
87 Ibid. 22.
88 Ibid. 26.
89 Ibid. 27.

faculties that demonstrates 'our absolute dependence upon a powerful Divine operation, for anything in us that hath a saving tendency'.[90]

God's use of means—afflictions in the case of Manasseh (see 2 Chron. 33) and the Gospel Word preached as in the case of Lydia (see Acts 16: 14)—all indicate that salvation is not the fruit of free will initiative but of God's sovereign 'good pleasure'.[91] Yet this does not reduce sinners to being blocks of stone or mere puppets on a string. Therefore, a proper grasp of the 'grace vs. free-will' dispute is essential. At this point, Calamy cites the opinions of two eminent 'Amyraldians', James Ussher and Jean Daillé that the Council of Orange (AD 529) provided the best decision 'in all antiquity' on this issue, viz. 'that it is from special grace, and the influence of the [Holy] Spirit, that any inclination is produced in the will of a corrupt creature towards God'.[92]

This last emphasis is developed in Calamy's fourth and final proposition. Obviously reflecting the 'free offer' theology of Calvin, Davenant and Baxter, Calamy is anxious to avoid the extremes[93] of Hypercalvinism and Arminianism.

> For though 'tis through special mercy, that any are recovered and saved, yet the mercy of God is so far exerted towards all, that He's ever before hand with them, and never stops the current of His favour towards them, till they obstinately reject the grace he offers, and wilfully abuse that common grace which had been afforded to them.[94]

For Calamy, this points the way to a proper balanced view of the Gospel:

> Let us put things together, and take notice, that general grace and special are very reconcilable; ... The Scripture appears clear as to both; and where's the inconsistency? Why must we deny general grace to exalt that which is special (as John Gill did later)? Or deny and depress special grace, to advance that which is general (as John Wesley did later)? ... *And is not this very consistent with our owning that 'God so loved the world' in general, as 'that He gave His only-begotten Son, that whosoever believeth in Him, might not perish, but might have everlasting life'?* And on the other side, is not general grace sufficiently secured by our maintaining God's love to the world, and His willing the salvation of all men, on condition they turn to Him? ... and why then should we go about to dash these truths against each other which are fairly consistent, and agree well together? Let us beware of extremes: and stand upon our guard, lest for fear of one error, we fall into another.[95]

---

90   Ibid. 28.
91   Ibid. 29–33.
92   Ibid. 34–5.
93   Ibid. 37.
94   Ibid. 40.
95   Ibid. 44–54 (emphasis mine).

Indeed, together with their disciples, ancient and modern, it would have done Gill and Wesley both good to have studied this sermon by Calamy!

Applying his carefully balanced exposition, Calamy concludes by warning against hypercalvinist inertia: 'Let us never pretend to open a way for the greater honour to the mercy of God, by indulging [in] negligence and sloth. That would be a 'turning the grace of our God into lasciviousness' (Jude 5).[96] Likewise he warns against Arminian self-congratulation: 'Let all such as heartily do will and run, thankfully adore that God that hath shewn mercy. Let them do so more earnestly, because of their natural aversion, which they cannot but have found and felt. With what ardour should you love Him that hath made you special objects of His favour'.[97] In short, by citing Philippians 1: 6 and Psalm 115: 1, Calamy insist that God has the 'entire glory' in our salvation.[98]

Lastly, Calamy is not content that we possess only an accurate 'head knowledge' of all he's argued for in this impressive sermon: 'Let us endeavour to get our hearts impressed with as deep a sense as may be, of the riches and freeness of [Divine mercy]'.[99] For those who feel paralysed in unbelief, our preacher provides a final exhortation:

> And therefore as thou canst, complain of thy spiritual deadness, stupidity, and enmity, and beg of God that he would cure it by His victorious grace. ... God ... had much rather His mercy should triumph in thy effectual 'willing' and 'running', till thou reachest everlasting salvation; than that His justice should be displayed, upon thy persisting in incurable hardness, in thy final ruin and destruction'.[100]

Such was the character and quality, the faithfulness and compassion of Dr Edmund Calamy's Gospel preaching. In the noble tradition of Richard Baxter, and anticipating the later contribution of Philip Doddridge, such teaching directed his faithful London ministry, conducted during the depressing days of the early eighteenth century.

---

96 Ibid. 45.
97 Ibid. 46.
98 Ibid.
99 Ibid. 47.
100 Ibid. 48.

By the same author

Alan C. Clifford, *Richard Baxter: The Gospel Truth* (Norwich: Charenton Reformed Publishing, 2016). ISBN 978–0–9929465–3–1

The chief characteristic, and main strength, of the book is its combination of commitment with scholarly rigour in setting Baxter in a wider context than is usual. Reading it, one gets a rich sense of his intellectual and religious context, his 'networks' and 'afterlife' as we say nowadays, and not only that, but the other characters in the cast list receive a respectful attention such as they do not usually attract. Alan Clifford has managed to write a book about Baxter that is individual, original, persuasive and thought provoking, distinctively his, and that is a rare thing.

Neil Keeble, Emeritus Professor of English Studies, University of Stirling

Academic

Richard Baxter: *Reliquiæ Baxterianæ*

Or, Mr Richard Baxter's Narrative of the Most Memorable Passages of his Life and Times

Edited by **N. H. Keeble**, **John Coffey**, **Tim Cooper**, and **Tom Charlton**

- The first scholarly edition of this work, presenting a full and reliable text, derived from the manuscript where this is extant

- Enables an accurate understanding and appreciation of this unique early modern text and primary historical source

- Includes full supporting editorial apparatus: textual, critical, expository, historical, and literary

- Reveals the wealth of Baxter's reference to hundreds of persons (many never before identified), historical sources and texts, and contemporary events

- Accompanied by extensive general and textual introductions

Dr. Edmund Calamy's Publications

Facsimiles of these can be found on Early English Books Online (EEBO) and Eighteenth Century Collections Online (ECCO) (for those with login credentials)

1.   Exercitationes Philosophicæ de Fictis Innutarum idearum mysteriis, Pars secunda, quam, favente Deo Opt. Max. sub præsidio M. Gerardi de Vries, Philosophiæ Doctoris, ejusdem facultatis in illustri Academia Ultrajectina Professoris Ordinarii publicè ventilandam proponit Edmundus Calamy, Londino-Anglus, ad diem 8 Decemb. horis locoque solitis.

Trajecti ad Rhenum [Utrecht] officina Francisci Halma, Academiæ typographi 1688.

2.   A Funeral Sermon, preached at the interment of Mr. Samuel Stevens, for some time employed in the work of the ministry in this city. 4to. London, 1694.

3.   A practical Discourse concerning vows, with a special reference to Baptism and the Lord's Supper, 8vo. 1694. Ed. 2, 12mo. 1704.

4.   A Funeral Sermon, preached upon occasion of the decease of the eminently pious Mrs. Elizabeth Williams, late wife of the Reverend Mr. Daniel Williams; with some account of her exemplary character, 8vo. 1698.

5.   A Sermon to the Societies for Reformation of manners in London and Middlesex. 12mo. 1699.

6.   A Discourse concerning the Rise and Antiquity of Cathedral Worship. Anon. 1699. [The EEBO webpage says this was actually written by Benjamin Calamy (1642–1686), the uncle of Dr. Edmund Calamy. The EEBO copy is missing pages 2 and 3.]

7.   An Abridgment of Mr. Baxter's History of his Life and Times. With an account of many others of those worthy Ministers, who were ejected after the Restauration of King Charles the Second; their apology for themselves, and their adherents, containing the grounds of their Nonconformity, and practice, as to stated and occasional communion with the Church of

England; and a continuation of their history till the year 1691. By Edmund Calamy, Edm. *Fil. et Nepos.* 8vo. 1702. Ed. 2, 1713, "in 2 volumes."

8.   Divine Mercy Exalted; or Free Grace in all its glory. Being a Sermon on Rom. ix. 16. Preached at the Merchants' Lecture at Salters' Hall, on Tuesday, October 20, 1702, by E. Calamy. *E. F. et N.* Published at the request of many encouragers of the Lecture. 8vo. 1703.

9.   A Defence of Moderate Nonconformity, in answer to the Reflections of Mr. Ollyffe and Mr. Hoadley, on the 10th chapter of the Abridgment of the Life of the Reverend Mr. Richard Baxter.

Part I. With a Postscript, containing some remarks on a Tract of Mr. Dorrington's, entitled, "The Dissenting Ministry in Religion, censored and condemned from the Holy Scriptures." 8vo. 1703.

10.   Part II. With an Introduction about the true state of the present controversy between the Church and Dissenters; and a Postscript, containing an answer to Mr. Hoadley's "Serious Admonition," and some remarks on a Letter of a nameless Author, said to be a Congregational Minister in the country. 8vo. 1704.

11.   Part III. To which are added three letters: one to Mr. Ollyffe, in answer to his "Second Defence of Ministerial Conformity;" another to Mr. Hoadley, in answer to his "Defence of the Reasonableness of Conformity;" and a third, to the author, from Mr. Rastrick, of Lynn, in Norfolk, giving an account of his Non-conformity. 8vo. 1705.

12.   A Funeral Sermon, occasioned by the sudden death of the Reverend Mr. Matthew Sylvester, preached at his meeting-house in Blackfriars. 8vo. 1708.

13.   A Funeral Sermon, occasioned by the much lamented death of Mrs. Frances Lewis, wife of Thomas Lewis, Esq.; who departed this life on February 9, 1707–8. Preached at Westminster on the Lord's Day following. 8vo. 1708.

14.   A Funeral Sermon, occasioned by the decease of Mr. Michael Watts, citizen and haberdasher of London. Preached at the meeting-house in Silver Street, the next Lord's Day after his interment. 8vo. 1708.

15.   A Caveat against New Prophets. In two Sermons at the Merchants' Lecture at Salters'-hall. 8vo. 1708.

16.   An Answer to Sir Richard Bulkeley's Remarks. Single sheet 8vo. 1708.

17.   A Sermon at the Merchants' Lecture in Salters'-hall, on December 7, 1708, upon occasion of the many late Bankrupts. 8vo. 1708.

18.   The Inspiration of the Holy Writings of the Old and New Testament, considered and improved. In fourteen Sermons, preached at the Merchants' Lecture at Salters'-hall. To which is added a single sermon, in vindication of the Divine Institution of the Office of the Ministry, preached at the same Lecture. 8vo. 1710.

19.   Comfort and Counsel to Protestant Dissenters; with some serious queries to such as hate and cast them out; and a friendly admonition to such as desert them. In two sermons, preached, first at Westminster, and afterwards at the Merchants' Lecture in Salters'-hall. 8vo. 1712.

20.   The Prudence of the Serpent and Innocence of the Dove. A Sermon, preached at Exeter, May 6, 1713, before a numerous assembly of the Dissenting ministers of Devon and Cornwall. Published at their common request. 8vo. 1713.

21.   Obadiah's Character; a sermon to young people. Preached in the Old Jewry. 8vo. 1713.

22.   Queries humbly proposed to my Lords the Bishops. Anon. 8vo. 1714.

23.   The Seasonableness of Religious Societies. A sermon preached to the supporters of the Lecture on Lord's Day Mornings, at Little St. Helen's. 8vo. 1714.

24.   God's Concern for his Glory in the British Isles; and the Security of Christ's Church from the Gates of Hell. In three Sermons, at the Merchants' Lecture in Salters'-hall. 8vo. 1715.

25. The Principles and Practice of moderate Non-conformists, with respect to Ordination, exemplified; in a Sermon, preached at the Ordination, Jan. 19, 1717; and a Charge given to Mr. James Read, Mr. Henry Read, Mr. Richard Briscoe, Mr. George Smyth, and Mr. Samuel Chandler, after their being ordained, December 19, 1716. To which is added, a Letter to a Divine in Germany, giving a brief but true account of the Dissenters in England. 8vo. 1717.

26.   Sober-mindedness recommended; in a Sermon, preached to a Society of Catechumens in Jewin-street. 8vo. 1717.

27.   The Repeal of the Act against Occasional Conformity considered; in a Letter to a member of the honourable House of Commons, October 1717.

28.   A Letter to Mr. Archdeacon Echard, upon occasion of his History of England; wherein the true principles of the Revolution are defended, the Whigs and Dissenters vindicated, several persons of distinction cleared from aspersions, and a number of historical mistakes rectified. 8vo. Ed. 2, corrected, 1718.

29.   The Church and Dissenters compared, as to Persecution; in some remarks on Dr. Walker's attempt to recover the names and sufferings of the Clergy that were sequestered, &c. between 1640 and 1660. 8vo. 1719.

30.   Discontented Complaints of the present times proved unreasonable; in a Sermon, preached at Rotherhithe, on the Anniversary of King George's Coronation. 8vo. 1720.

31.   A Charge given to Mr. Obadiah Hughes, Mr. Clerk Oldisworth, Mr. Thomas Newman, and Mr. John Smith, after their Ordination in the Old Jewry. 8vo. 1721.

32.   Thirteen Sermons concerning the doctrine of the Trinity. Preached at the Merchants' Lecture at Salter's Hall. Together with a vindication of that celebrated text, 1 John v. 7, from being spurious; and an explication of it, upon the supposition of its being genuine. In four Sermons, preached at the same Lecture. An. 1719, 1720. 8vo. 1722.

33.   The Ministry of the Dissenters vindicated; in an Ordination Sermon, preached at Aylesbury, in the county of Bucks. Added to Ed. 2. A Letter to the author of a pamphlet, intitled, "The Ministry of the Dissenters proved to be null and void, from Scripture and antiquity." 8vo. 1724.

34.   Memoirs of the Life of the late Reverend Mr. John Howe. 8vo. 1724.

35.   The Word of God the Young Man's best Directory; a Sermon, preached to a Society of young men in Silver Street, on the birth-day of his Majesty King George.

36.   A Charge given to Mr. William Hunt, after his Ordination at Newport Pagnel, in the county of Bucks. 8vo. 1725.

37.   A Funeral Sermon for the late Reverend Mr. John Sheffield, Minister of the Gospel, in Southwark, who departed this life, January 24, 1726. *Ann. ætat.* 73. 8vo. 1726.

38.   A Funeral Sermon for the late Mr. Joseph Bennet, Minister of the Gospel, in the Old Jewry, who departed this life, February 2, 1726, *An. ætat.* 61. 8vo. 1726.

39.   A continuation of the Account of the Ministers, Lecturers, Masters, and Fellows of Colleges, and Schoolmasters, who were ejected and silenced, after the Restoration in 1660, by, or before the Act for Uniformity. To which is added, The Church and Dissenters, compared as to persecution, and also, some free remarks on the 28th chapter of Dr. Bennet's Essay on the Thirty-nine Articles of Religion. In two volumes 8vo. 1727.

40. A Funeral Sermon for the late Rev. Mr. Mottershed, Minister of the Gospel, in Ratcliffe, who departed this life, October 13, 1728. *An. ætat* 63. 8vo. 1728.

41. Gospel Ministers, the Salt of the Earth, being a sermon, [on *Mat.* v. 13,] preached to Ministers of the three Denominations, in and about the cities of London and Westminster, in the Public Library of Dr. Daniel Williams, situated in Red Cross-street, in the parish of St. Giles Cripplegate, on October 28, 1731. By Edmund Calamy, DD.

The following reset volumes can be downloaded from quintapress.com (follow the PDF Books link)

An Abridgement Mr Baxter's History of his Life and Times, first edition (1702)

An Abridgement Mr Baxter's History of his Life and Times, second edition, Volume 1 (1713)

An Account of the Ministers, Lecturers, Masters and Fellows of Colleges and Schoolmasters, who were ejected or Silenced after the Restoration in 1660. By, or before, the Act of Uniformity, second edition, Volume 2 (1713)

A Continuation of the Account of the Ministers, Lecturers, Masters and Fellows of Colleges and Schoolmasters, who were ejected or Silenced after the Restoration in 1660 by or before the Act of Uniformity, Volume 1 (1727)

A Continuation of the Account of the Ministers, Lecturers, Masters and Fellows of Colleges and Schoolmasters, who were ejected or Silenced after the Restoration in 1660 by or before the Act of Uniformity, Volume 2 (1727)

God's Concern for his Glory in the British Isles; and The Security of Christ's Church from the Gates of Hell (1715)

A Practical Discourse Concerning Vows: with a Special Reference to Baptism and the Lord's Supper (1697)

A Funeral Sermon, preached Upon Occasion of the Decease of Mrs. Elizabeth Williams (1698)

A Funeral Sermon, preached at the Interment of Mr Samuel Stephens (1694)

CENTER *for* BAPTIST STUDIES
at THE SOUTHERN BAPTIST THEOLOGICAL SEMINARY

The Andrew Fuller Center for Baptist Studies, located at
The Southern Baptist Theological Seminary in Louisville,
Kentucky, seeks to promote the study of Baptist history as well
as theological reflection on the contemporary significance of
that history. The center is named in honor of Andrew Fuller
(1754–1815), the late eighteenth- and early nineteenth-century
English Baptist pastor and theologian, who played a key
role in opposing aberrant thought in his day as well as being
instrumental in the founding and early years of the Baptist
Missionary Society. Fuller was a close friend and theological
mentor of William Carey, one of the pioneers of that society.

The Andrew Fuller Center holds an annual two-day
conference in September that examines various aspects
of Baptist history and thought. It also supports the
publication of the critical edition of the Works of Andrew
Fuller, and from time to time, other works in Baptist
history. The Center seeks to play a role in the mentoring
of junior scholars interested in studying Baptist history.

andrewfullercenter.org

H&E Publishing is a Canadian evangelical publishing company located out of Peterborough, Ontario. We exist to provide Christ-exalting, Gospel-centred, and Bible-saturated content aimed to show God to be as glorious and worthy as He truly is.

hesedandemet.com